MAKE YOUR OWN WILL

IN THE BACK POCKET:

Why make a will?

Making a will allows you to set out who should enjoy the benefit of your worldly wealth after your death. If there are people who depend on you financially, their well-being may depend on whether or not you have left a will. Yet many people put off making a will because it appears too complicated, or it involves a visit to a solicitor or they do not want to think about their death.

This Action Pack takes you step by step through drawing up a will, setting out the decisions you must make. It explains what you must do in plain English and highlights some of the pitfalls to be avoided. It also includes simple will forms that you can use to draw up your own will – something most people can do without difficulty.

But don't try to draw up your own will if any of the following applies to you:

- you have been married more than once
- you want to do anything more than divide your property among a few people
- your estate will be liable to inheritance tax (see Section 3)
- you will be providing for someone with physical or mental disabilities
- you own a business or farm (or a substantial holding in a private company)
- you want to pass on your home with conditions attached
- you were born abroad or are likely to be considered domiciled outside England and Wales
- you are involved with family trusts.

It can also pay to get professional advice if your estate might be liable to inheritance tax. With tax at 40%, a small saving in tax would easily cover the cost of consulting a professional adviser.

If any of these applies to you, use the Pack to help you work out what you are worth, what inheritance tax could mean for your estate and what you hope to achieve with your will. Then take the paperwork to a solicitor for professional advice on drawing up the will itself.

If you don't leave a will

If you die without leaving a will *(intestate)*, what you leave will be divided up and distributed among your family and close relatives according to the legal rules of intestacy. The rules for distributing any property you leave not covered by a valid will in England and Wales are illustrated in the diagram opposite.

In some cases, the result of intestacy may be just what you would have wanted if you had written a will. But if you die leaving a husband or wife or young children, the laws of intestacy could make their life more difficult than if you had left a will.

In some cases, none of your estate might go to the person you would most want to have it. Anyone you have been living with who is not your husband or wife or a close relative would be entitled to nothing under the rules of intestacy (though they might be able to claim something – see Box opposite).

A further complication with an intestate estate is that you can't have any say in how it will be dealt with. An administrator is appointed – usually your surviving spouse or nearest relative if he or she is prepared to do the job, but this person may not be your first choice to look after your affairs after your death.

And if anything goes to children under the age of 18, it will be put in trust until they reach 18 or marry, if earlier. It will be administered according to the strict rules of trust law, giving very little scope for your trustees to use their discretion.

Lastly, if you don't leave a will, you can lose the chance to minimise the inheritance tax payable on your estate. With the rate of tax now at 40% on taxable transfers in excess of £231,000 in total, this could be costly.

Other things in a will

You can use your will to express preferences for:

- who will look after any children you will leave – you can appoint guardians for children under 18
- cremation or burial (and where) – though while it is usual to respect your wishes, there is no legal obligation to do so
- donating organs or your body for medical purposes – call the Organ Donation Literature Line (0845 6060 400) for details.

Who your money would go to if you died without making a will (in England & Wales)

Do you have a wife or husband?

YES

- is your estate worth more than £125,000?
  - **NO** → wife/husband gets everything
  - **YES** → do you have children?
    - **YES** → wife/husband gets the chattels and first £125,000 plus life interest in half the rest – the balance goes to children
    - **NO** → do you have parents/ brothers and sisters?
      - **YES** → wife/husband gets first £200,000 plus half the rest – the balance goes to your parents (brothers and sisters if both parents are dead)
      - **NO** → wife/husband gets everything

NO

- do you have children?
  - **YES** → shared equally between children
  - **NO** → do you have parents?
    - **YES** → shared equally between parents
    - **NO** → do you have brothers and sisters?
      - **YES** → shared equally between brothers and sisters
      - **NO** → do you have grandparents?
        - **YES** → shared equally between grandparents
        - **NO** → do you have uncles and aunts?
          - **YES** → shared equally between uncles and aunts or their children if uncles and aunts have died
          - **NO** → everything goes to the Crown

NOTES:

[1] Adopted and illegitimate children are treated as legitimate. Relatives who are descended from the same pair of ancestors as the dead person will inherit before any relative who only shares one common ancestor – e.g. half-brothers and sisters.

[2] As a general rule, if a relative who would have inherited dies before you, his or her share is divided equally between his or her children. For example, any children – your grandchildren – would inherit his or her share.

[3] 'Children' does not include stepchildren.

[4] The wife or husband always gets the personal effects – e.g. furniture, car – as well as any money they are entitled to.

[5] If you share ownership of a house with your wife or husband (or anyone else) through a joint tenancy (see page 9), your share automatically goes to the co-owner. With a tenancy in common, your share of the house is distributed with the rest of your estate according to the rules above.

[6] If one spouse survives the other by fewer than 28 days, the survivor will not take an interest under the intestacy of the first to die.

What happens if you overlook your family or other dependants

It has been known for people to leave close family out of their wills – either deliberately or through forgetfulness. And with the increase in divorce, there may be more than one set of people expecting a share of your estate. Under the Inheritance (Provision for Family and Dependants) Act 1975, some relatives, co-habitees of at least two years and anyone who can prove that they were partly or wholly maintained by someone who has just died can claim reasonable provision from the estate. This also applies where no will is left.

However, the procedure for claiming is complicated and uncertain, and could be costly. It's better to think it all out clearly in advance to avoid such a situation.

Since 1984 it has been possible for the beneficiaries of a will (or intestacy) to vary the dispositions of the will after the death, providing the beneficiaries are all over 18, the variation is made within two years of the death and it is notified to the Inland Revenue. As it should be in writing and as there are several conditions to observe, help should be obtained from a solicitor.

What do you own?

The first step in drawing up a will is to work out just what you (and your husband or wife if you are married) are worth. This tells you what you've got to dispose of, and whether you should be worrying about inheritance tax. Worksheet A in the back pocket is designed to help you work out how much you're worth. There's space to give details about where each item is kept or where accounts are held: if you keep it with your will, it should make the job of carrying it out much easier.

For most people, their house will probably be the biggest part of their wealth. If you are the sole owner, its value will be what you could get for it if you sold it today (before paying the estate agent, solicitors etc.), less any mortgage or loans outstanding on it. If you share ownership of the house with someone else (under a joint tenancy or tenancy in common), then its value is your share of what you would get by selling it today, less any mortgage or loans *you* owe on it.

Illustrated, opposite, is how a typical couple might fill in Worksheet A. If your affairs are complicated or if you have lots of different investments, there won't be enough room for all the details. Draw up the information on a series of separate sheets of paper (one for each category) and enter the totals on the Worksheet.

As well as helping you and your executors in working out what your estate comprises, completing Worksheet A will tell you whether you need to consider inheritance tax. You need not worry about this tax if you can answer YES to ALL of the following three questions:

1 Are you worth less than £231,000 in total (including, if you are married, what your husband or wife is worth)?

2 Have you given away less than £3,000 each year in gifts during the past seven years (ignore gifts to your husband or wife and gifts under £250)?

3 Are the answers to questions 1 and 2 still likely to be YES in seven years' time?

If you say NO to any of these three questions, then you need to read the next section; otherwise you can skip it and go on to Section 4.

Note that you should check what you are worth every year or two or whenever your circumstances change. For example, changes in house prices can easily alter what you are worth very quickly.

Check your life insurance

While you're working out just what would be left on your death, use the opportunity to review your life insurance. You may already be adequately covered by life insurance provided as a fringe benefit at work or through policies linked to your mortgage. If not, term insurance is the cheapest way to buy life insurance cover until the children are independent.

If you belong to a pension scheme which is written in trust, make sure that the trustees know who you would wish to benefit from any lump sum paid out on your death. The trustees will normally have complete discretion about who gets the money (this means no inheritance tax on it – see page 6), but they will usually respect your wishes. You need to be clear which policies pay out to your estate and which are held in trust.

How Michael and Mary Smith complete Worksheet A

The Smiths begin by entering the value of their home: it's worth around £200,000 with a £30,000 mortgage outstanding – £170,000 to be divided between them since the home is jointly owned. They itemise their savings, investments and valuables, each adding £5,000 for the value of furniture and effects which they value at approximately £10,000.

Michael has life insurance cover at work, of four times his salary of £30,000; Mary is covered by a term insurance policy worth £50,000.

The Smiths deduct the total of outstanding loans and find that Michael's estate alone is worth more than the £231,000 limit for considering inheritance tax, so he might wish to create a trust for his insurance policy to take it out of his estate.

WORKSHEET

A

MAKE YOUR OWN WILL – AN ACTION PACK FROM WHICH?

WHAT DO YOU OWN?

Divide property held jointly with your spouse appropriately

DATE 22/03/99	Self £	Spouse £ (if married)	Location of documents
HOME (market value with vacant possession less outstanding mortgages)	85,000	85,000	SLAGTHORPE BUILDING SOCIETY
OTHER HOMES OR LAND	—	—	
MONEY (including interest earned) **IN**:	600		ALL FILED IN
the bank		2,000	CONCERTINA FILE
National Savings		1,000	IN LOCKED
building society		10,000	DESK DRAWER
other deposits			
INVESTMENTS:			
stocks and shares	—	—	
TESSAs	3,000	3,000	
unit trusts	—	30,000	DITTO
PEPs/ISAs	50,000	—	
LIFE INSURANCE amounts to be paid out including any bonuses (unless written in trust)	120,000	50,000	CONCERTINA FILE (UNDER 'INSURANCE')
VALUABLES antiques, jewellery, etc.	1,000 ①	2,000 ②	① WATERCOLOURS ② JEWELLERY
OTHER FURNITURE AND EFFECTS total second-hand value	5,000	5,000	
CAR(S) FORD ESCORT	7,000	—	CONCERTINA FILE (UNDER 'CAR')
OTHER POSSESSIONS (e.g. caravan, dinghy)	—	—	
LOANS – money you are owed	—	—	
BUSINESS/FARM VALUE	—	—	
INTERESTS IN TRUSTS OR SETTLEMENTS (i.e. any rights you have to income, capital or property held in trust)	—	—	
TOTAL	271,600	188,000	
DEDUCT: outstanding loans (exclude mortgages, which you took into account under 'Home').	5,000 400		BANK LOAN (UNDER 'BANK') TV/VIDEO (UNDER 'HP')
FUNERAL EXPENSES (estimate)	1,500	1,500	
VALUE OF ESTATE NOW	264,700	186,500	

Inheritance tax

Inheritance tax is the only tax payable on the value of what you leave when you die. It replaced capital transfer tax in 1986 and covers what you leave on death and anything you have given away in the previous seven years. Anything given away outright more than seven years before your death is normally free of inheritance tax (unless it is given to certain types of trust or a company).

In this section we give a brief guide to inheritance tax on your death. If after reading it you feel that you need more detailed information, be sure to take professional advice – see page 10.

What is taxable

When you die, everything you own outright – home, possessions, investments and savings – goes into your estate. This includes money paid out by life insurance policies unless they are 'written in trust' for someone else (see page 10). Debts (including outstanding mortgages) and funeral expenses (including the cost of a memorial stone) are deducted to give the net value of your estate.

You won't necessarily have to pay tax on the whole value: some of your bequests and legacies may be exempt from inheritance tax – see Box below. For example, anything left to your husband or wife is exempt from tax, as are gifts to charity. These exempt bequests and legacies are therefore deducted from the value of your estate before the tax bill is worked out.

Then any gifts made to other people in the seven years before your death which are not exempt from tax (see Box, below) are added. If the resulting total exceeds a certain limit (£231,000 for 1999-2000), inheritance tax is payable on the amount over that limit.

Note that if you make gifts to certain types of trust you may have to pay inheritance tax at the time of the gift. And gifts of this type made more than seven years before your death can also affect the tax payable on your death. If you are involved with trusts, be sure to get professional advice about inheritance tax (what follows does not deal with these gifts).

And if you have given something away but still retain the right to use it (or any benefit from it), this may be treated as a 'gift with reservation'. The value of it can be added to your estate – if this is likely to bring it over the £231,000 limit for paying inheritance tax, consider seeking professional advice.

For example, if a man gives his house to his children, but continues to live in it without payment, the gift will still attract inheritance tax.

Tax-free gifts

Gifts that are always free of inheritance tax

- Gifts between husband and wife (though if the person who gets the gift isn't domiciled in the UK only the first £55,000 of gifts is free of tax)
- Gifts to UK registered charities
- Gifts to certain national institutions (e.g. the National Trust, British Museum)
- Gifts of certain types of heritage property to a non-profit-making body – see page 14
- Gifts of land in the UK to a registered housing association on or after 14 March 1989

Gifts free of inheritance tax on death only

- Lump-sum payments from pension schemes provided that the trustees of the scheme have total discretion about who gets the money (they usually do)
- Refunds of personal pension plan premiums (and interest) provided that they are paid directly to someone else or in trust (i.e. are not paid out to the personal representatives)
- The estate of a person whose death was caused or hastened by active or military service in war or of a warlike nature
- Lump sums paid out by life insurance policies written in trust for someone else.

The tax due

The tax due on your taxable estate and on any taxable gifts you made in the seven years before your death is worked out as follows:

1 First work out the tax due (if any) on the earliest taxable gift, using the rates in Table 1.

2 Now add the next earliest gift to the earliest gift, and work out how much tax is due on the running total, using the rates in Table 1. Subtract the tax due on the earliest gift from the tax due on the total to find the tax due on the next earliest gift.

3 Add each subsequent gift to the running total in the same way and find out the tax due on the new running total. Subtract from this the tax due on the previous gifts to find the tax due on this gift.

4 Lastly, add the total value of your taxable estate to the running total and find out the tax due on this final running total. Subtract from this the tax due on all the previous gifts to find the tax due on your estate.

5 The tax due on any gifts made between three and seven years before death is reduced, on the scale in Table 2.

Gifts free of inheritance tax in your lifetime only

- Small gifts of up to £250 to any number of different people in any one tax year
- Gifts made as normal expenditure out of income (i.e. not by drawing on capital) – see page 9
- Gifts on marriage – each parent can give £5,000 tax free in anticipation of the marriage, a grand-parent or great-grandparent £2,500 and anyone else £1,000 (conditional on the marriage taking place)
- Certain gifts for the maintenance of your family (e.g. an ex-husband or ex-wife, children under 18 or in full-time education or infirm relatives)
- Up to £3,000 a year on other gifts (any unused part of this allowance can be carried over to the next tax year only).

The rates of tax

The thresholds for inheritance tax may change – and there have been more than two rates of tax in the past. When the tax due on a gift or bequest is being calculated, the rates in force at the time of the giver's death (not at the time of the gift) apply.

Table 1
Rates of inheritance tax for 1999-2000

Taxable gifts	Rate of tax
£0 – £231,000	nil %
£231,000 or more	40% of the excess

Table 2
Tax on gifts made before death

Years between gift and death	Percentage of the full charge payable
Up to 3	100%
More than 3 and up to 4	80%
More than 4 and up to 5	60%
More than 5 and up to 6	40%
More than 6 and up to 7	20%

Valuing your possessions

Everything you leave on death or give away in the seven years before you die (except tax-exempt gifts) must be valued to work out your inheritance tax bill.

You need to know the current value or, in the case of gifts, the value at the date of the gift.

The general rule is that the value is the price you could get for the asset if it was sold on the open

Example 1

Joe Soap died in May 1999 leaving an estate worth £200,000 to his children. He had given away a total of £80,000 just over five years before his death, and no other taxable gifts before then. Two annual exemptions of £3,000 could be deducted.

The earliest taxable gift was therefore £74,000, on which tax is due at nil% – i.e. no tax to pay. There were no other taxable gifts made in Joe's lifetime, so the value of his taxable estate (£200,000) is added to the running total of £74,000 to give a total of £274,000.

The inheritance tax due is calculated as follows:

The first £231,000 is taxed at nil%	£0
The next £43,000 is taxed at 40%	£17,200
Total tax	£17,200

Since no tax was due on the £80,000 of gifts made in Joe's lifetime, all of this £17,200 inheritance tax bill is due on his estate.

Example 2

Alan Easy dies in May 1999, leaving the whole of his estate worth £150,000 to his daughter, Meg. He made gifts of £120,000 to his son Peter in January 1995 and £140,000 to his son James in January 1996.

Upon Alan's death his executors have to calculate the liability to inheritance tax by adding together the gifts made in the seven years before his death (after deducting allowable exemptions) and the value of his estate on his death.

The 1995 annual allowance of £3,000 and the unused 1994 annual allowance of £3,000 (which can be carried forward) can be set off against Peter's gift, leaving £114,000 of his gift potentially liable to tax.

Because the 1995 annual allowance has already been utilised, only the 1996 annual allowance can be offset against James's gift, leaving £137,000 potentially liable to tax.

1 The earliest gift in the seven years before Alan's death is the £120,000 to Peter, of which £114,000 is potentially liable to tax, but, as this is still under the £231,000 threshold, no tax is payable.

2 The next gift is the £140,000 to James in January 1996, of which £137,000 is potentially liable to tax. This is added to the £114,000 of Peter's gift to produce a running total of £251,000, which is liable to tax. Tax on this sum is calculated as follows:

The first £231,000 is taxed at nil%	£0
The next £20,000 is taxed at 40%	£8,000
Total tax on £251,000 (originally £260,000)	£8,000

No tax was due on the first £120,000 gift, so all of this £8,000 is charged on James's gift. The tax bill will be further reduced because the gift was made more than three years before Alan's death (see 4).

3 The only other taxable amount is the £150,000 estate which Alan left to Meg. When this is added, the running total of taxable gifts and estate amounts to £401,000. Tax on this total is calculated thus:

The first £231,000 is taxed at nil%	£0
The next £170,000 is taxed at 40%	£68,000
Total tax on £401,000	£68,000

The tax due on the first £260,000 of gifts was £8,000, so the tax due on Alan's estate (the last £150,000) is £68,000 *less* £8,000 = £60,000.

4 The £60,000 tax due on the £150,000 left to Meg is payable in full out of her legacy, so she gets £150,000 *less* £60,000 = £90,000. James's £140,000 (£137,000 liable to tax) gift was made more than three years, but less than four years, before Alan's death, so the tax payable is 80% of the full charge of £8,000 – i.e. £6,400 (which has to be paid by James). No tax is due on Peter's gift.

market. With things like cars and personal possessions, this is the second-hand value. The value of stocks and shares quoted on the Stock Exchange depends on the prices at which they were traded on the day.

There are special ways of valuing unquoted shares, life interests and family businesses. If you're involved with these, you should take professional advice on valuing these and all aspects of drawing up your will.

Minimising inheritance tax

If some inheritance tax is likely to be due on your estate, you can help reduce the tax bill by giving as much as possible away before you die. But never give away so much that you or your spouse are left impoverished in old age. Remember that your heirs will still be better off even if they have to pay tax.

Gifts made more then seven years before you die are free of inheritance tax altogether (unless made with reservation, or to certain types of trust or a company). But you can also minimise the tax due on gifts made during the seven years before you die by using the exemptions which enable you to make tax-free gifts. And the tax bill on gifts made more than three years before you die is reduced (see Table 2).

For example, you could make tax-free gifts out of your normal (i.e. after-tax) income, provided they are part of your regular spending. You must not draw on capital to make the gifts, and you should be able to demonstrate that you can keep up your usual standard of living after making the gifts. This exemption could cover the premiums on a life insurance policy written in trust for someone else (a child, for example): the proceeds of the policy on death would be paid straight to the beneficiary free of inheritance tax.

You can give an unlimited number of people small gifts of up to £250 (each year). You won't need to use this exemption if the gift is tax-free for another reason. But if you give more than £250 to anyone, in any one tax year, this exemption for that person is lost as an addition to the annual exemption of £3,000.

The £3,000 of gifts which can be made each year free of inheritance tax on top of other exempt gifts would allow you to give away £21,000 over a seven-year period without paying tax. If you give away less than £3,000 in any year, you can add the shortfall to the limit for the next tax year only.

Giving away things other than cash during your lifetime could mean a capital gains tax bill, although there are special provisions for businesses and farms. For example, if you gave away valuable jewellery, this could count as a disposal for capital gains tax purposes. The first £7,100 of taxable gains in the 1999-2000 tax year is free of tax but anything over this is taxed at the appropriate income tax rates.

Husband and wife

Gifts between husband and wife are exempt from inheritance tax, and each partner is entitled to his or her exempt gifts and nil rate band. Each can also make £7,100 of taxable gains without paying capital gains tax. So an important plank in tax planning is for husband and wife to share their wealth so that both can make tax-free gifts to other people.

For example, if you are worth £300,000, and leave your estate to your spouse, there would be no inheritance tax to pay on your death. But when your spouse died, leaving the £300,000, the tax at 1999-2000 rates would come to £27,600. If you split the money equally with your spouse and each of you passed your £150,000 direct to your children, there would be no tax to pay on either estate.

In practice it may not be so easy to split your wealth and give it away during your lifetime if the survivor is to have enough to live on. But the principle of sharing some of your wealth with your spouse and leaving some property direct to the next generation in order to take advantage of your own exempt band is worth considering.

Both spouses should make wills at the same time to ensure sensible co-ordination and tax planning.

A shared home

There are two ways of sharing ownership of a home: joint tenancy and tenancy in common (the term 'tenancy' here does not mean that you rent the home). If you share the ownership of a home at the time of your death, what happens to the home depends on the type of ownership.

If your home is jointly owned with someone else under a *joint tenancy*, you share the ownership of the whole home (neither of you can dispose of your own share without the other's agreement, although either can compel the sale of the whole in order to get his or her share). If one of you dies, ownership of the home as a whole automatically goes to the survivor, whatever your wills say.

If the joint tenancy is with your spouse, there will be no inheritance tax to pay, since what is left to a husband or wife is tax-free. With a joint tenancy of two people who are not married to each other – a mother and daughter or cohabitees, for example – the half of the tenancy which is automatically transferred to the survivor counts as part of your estate.

If the home is jointly owned as a *tenancy in common*, you each own a share of the value of the home and can dispose of your share to whomever you wish (or to more than one person). For example, you could bequeath part of your share to your spouse, and the other part to the next generation. This would reduce the eventual size of your spouse's estate, and, provided the next generation didn't want to sell their share, allow the spouse to continue living there. If they did want their share, they could force a sale of the whole. This scheme can create problems so take legal advice first.

You can change from a joint tenancy to a tenancy in common simply by giving written notice to your joint tenant. Changing the other way is less easy – seek legal advice if you want to do this.

Estate freezing

Estate freezing uses various techniques for 'freezing' the value of some of your wealth now and allowing the increase in value which would otherwise come to you to benefit someone else.

For example, investments can be put into trust for your children or grandchildren, reducing the value of your estate and allowing growth to accumulate in the trust. If you expect your wealth to grow over the next few years, this is worth considering – provided you don't need the money for yourself.

Get professional advice on how to set up trusts and drawing up your will once they are set up. You cannot retain any interest in the fund if you are seeking inheritance tax exemption.

Life insurance

Life insurance can help with inheritance tax in several ways. For example, *whole life insurance* policies pay out when you die (whenever this is) and could pay any inheritance tax due on your estate. The current rules mean that farms and businesses may pass without an inheritance tax charge, but the rules are not simple, so take specialist advice.

Large gifts in your lifetime could also mean an inheritance tax bill if you die within seven years of the gift. Special *term insurance* policies aim to provide enough to cover the bill if you die during this period.

Paying the premiums for a life insurance policy for someone else's benefit will not be a taxable gift if you can afford to pay them out of your normal after-tax income.

If you use life insurance to help with inheritance tax planning, ask the company to write the policy in trust for your beneficiaries. That way, the money is paid directly to them: it does not go into your estate and no inheritance tax is due on it.

Professional advice

If your estate could exceed £231,000 and you want to minimise inheritance tax, it is probably worth seeking professional tax-planning advice from a solicitor or accountant. This is especially true if you want to do any of the following:

- pass on a family home with strings attached to anyone other than your spouse, especially where the tax due will probably be more than the value of the rest of the estate
- pass on a family business or farm
- keep your tax bill to the barest minimum by sophisticated planning (e.g. setting up trusts).

Don't start cooking up crafty wheezes of your own to cut tax – there are tough rules to catch out the unwary. You could end up making things worse for those you leave behind.

Even if you're going to take professional advice, it is still worth reading on – it will help you make decisions which may have a bearing on your tax-planning strategy.

Executors

Your will is carried out or executed by the executors you name. They can also be called 'personal representatives'. It will be their task to 'prove' your will (called *getting probate*). They have to find out what you have left (and where), handle your investments, sell property where necessary or advisable, distribute your legacies and bequests, repay your debts, pay funeral expenses and taxes and otherwise wind up your estate.

You can appoint up to four executors to carry out the instructions in your will (if you appoint more than four, only four will be allowed to act). One executor would be enough for a simple will (with everything going to that person, say). But it is probably advisable to think about at least two – if only to have a substitute if one dies or cannot act for some other reason. There should be two executors if anyone under 18 is likely to benefit under the will.

It is common to appoint the person who has the biggest stake in the will as an executor – your spouse or an adult child, for example. The second executor is often a close friend who can share the burden (it is helpful if he or she is used to dealing with money or legal matters). Whoever you choose, check that the person is prepared to do the job – no one can be made to do it.

You can appoint a professional adviser such as a solicitor or accountant as executor (though professionals may insist on a professionally drawn-up will). They will charge fees for their work, payable out of the residue of the estate (at the rate when the will is carried out, not the rate when you draw it up).

Banks will also act as executors (and have the advantage of continuing to exist even if individual members of staff die or move on). But the charges are likely to be much higher (e.g. £4,000 on a gross estate of £100,000, plus yearly charges of around 1 per cent of the value of any trusts to be administered). And a bank will not always be able to give you the personal attention of a friend or adviser.

Though expensive for small estates or straightforward wills, a professional executor may be worthwhile if your will is complicated, if your affairs are tangled or if there are trusts to be set up or administered. If you are appointing professional advisers, the will should contain provision to pay them.

Once you have decided on your executors, enter them on Worksheet B in the back pocket. This is a checklist of the decisions you need to make when drawing up a will.

If you have expressed your preferences in your will about burial or cremation, tell your executors in case the will is not read until after the funeral.

Further information on this subject is available in a Which? Consumer Guide, **Wills and Probate**, price £10.99.

The book also explains to anyone called upon to act as an executor the procedure for getting probate granted. It includes sections on how to calculate assets, getting and filling in probate forms, carrying out valuations, dealing with the bank, paying inheritance tax and dealing with income and capital gains tax. It also tells you what to do after probate has been granted.

For how to order see page 28.

If you have children under 18

If you have children under the age of 18 (including adopted children and stepchildren if you are the legal guardian), there are two important decisions to make in drawing up your will:

- who you want to be the guardian if both parents die (if only one dies, the other automatically becomes guardian)
- where the money to look after them will come from.

If the parents are not married, the father should acquire 'parental responsibility' by agreement or court order if he wishes to appoint a guardian.

Note that if you have children under 18 from a previous marriage, it would be advisable to take professional advice in drawing up your will (but keep reading – this Pack will help you get the best out of your adviser).

Guardians

The first decision to be made is on the guardianship of children under 18 if they are left with no parents.

A guardian may often look after the children himself or herself. But if this is not possible or desirable, the guardian is responsible for deciding who does – with the legal right to determine questions such as the home, education and marriage of children until they reach the age of 18.

Choose a guardian (or guardians) you are confident will bring up your children in the way you would wish. Make sure that whoever you appoint is willing to take on the job – and provide for them in the will if necessary. There's space on Worksheet B to enter your choices, but make it clear what money they can keep and what money is on trust.

Resources

The second decision is on how to provide for your minor children financially if both of you die. If children under 18 inherit money and property, it is held in trust for them. Unless you make recommendations in your will about the administration of what you leave, it will be dealt with according to the rules set out in the trustee laws:

- after administering your will your executors will act as trustees of what you leave on behalf of the beneficiaries (your children)
- any houses or land will usually be sold, and the estate turned into cash or suitable investments
- at least half the money held on trust must be invested in certain safe investments such as British Government stock, National Savings and interest-bearing accounts unless wider powers are given in the will – the rest can be invested in other, possibly riskier, investments such as quoted shares, provided appropriate advice is taken.
- the income from the trust must be spent only for the maintenance, education and benefit of the children
- each child becomes entitled to his or her share of the trust on reaching the age of 18 (or when they marry if earlier)
- the trustees can advance half the share of the capital to which each child will be entitled at 18 before that age for the maintenance, education or benefit of that child.

These strict rules are designed to protect the interests of minor children. Professionally drawn-up wills usually give more freedom to the trustees – especially to keep inherited property (such as the family house), to invest in a wider selection of investments and to advance more than half the capital. Many wills also contain *stricter* rules on when the children get their share of the trust, leaving it to 21.

If you want to give your trustees more freedom, you should set out the extra powers you wish them to have in the will. Our yellow will form allows you to give the trustees the extra powers mentioned above when leaving money to your children under 18.

Bequests and legacies

Most wills follow a fairly simple pattern, including some or all of the following:

- a few bequests of treasured objects and possessions
- some cash legacies to special people and/or children
- everything else (the 'residue') to a single person or charity, or to be divided between more than one.

Use Worksheet B to list your bequests and legacies – there is guidance below on the options open to you.

Possessions

You can bequeath heirlooms, valued or treasured objects or any other possessions to particular individuals – your family wedding ring, for example, to a granddaughter, or fishing rods to the boy next door.

Enter the details necessary to identify the bequest and who is to get it on Worksheet B – this could help your executors. If there is any chance of confusion, describe the object carefully ('my red Austin 7') and give the full name and address of the recipient.

If there are a lot of possessions you want to give to particular people, you could leave them to a relative or friend (or an executor) to distribute. For example, after bequeathing the most valuable items, you may well say: 'The remainder of the contents of my house to Mary Morgan to dispose of as she sees fit'. Give Mary Morgan a list of who you would like to get the various items – she doesn't have to stick to it, but if you've chosen the right person, she will do so.

Money

You can leave sums of money in your will to particular people in several ways:

- fixed sums to named individuals – for example, '£100 to Joseph Soap and £50 to Meg Evans' (give their addresses)
- fixed sums to each group of individuals – for example '£500 to each of my brothers and sisters living at my death'.
- a fixed sum to be divided among a group of individuals – for example '£1,000 to be divided equally between all my grandchildren living at my death'.

Again, when filling in Worksheet B, give the fullest detail needed to avoid confusion (for example, a list of your brothers and sisters and their addresses if they are all to get legacies could avoid any delay while the executors trace them). If there are complications over a group (for example, does 'unmarried grandchildren' include those who are divorced or widowed?), it's best to leave a series of individual legacies to named individuals.

Note: anything left to your 'children' will include adopted children and illegitimate children but will not include stepchildren unless you specify otherwise.

If the beneficiary dies first

If you leave a bequest or a legacy to someone who dies before you, what you've left normally falls into the residue unless you've specified an alternative ('or, if he predeceases me, to Gordon Green...'). But if the beneficiary who dies before you is your child, whatever you've left is automatically divided between his or her children (your grandchildren by that child). It is still better to set this out in your will.

Who pays the tax on your bequests and legacies?

Anything left to your husband or wife is free of inheritance tax, but bequests and legacies to other people may be liable to tax. Tax due on a legacy or bequest is usually paid out of the residue of the estate – a 'tax-free' gift. But you can specify in your will that the recipient is to pay the tax out of the value of a bequest or legacy making it 'after-tax'.

You can't easily predict the tax bill on a bequest or legacy because it depends on the size of your estate, other gifts made in the years before you die and the tax rates in force at the time you die. So if you want the recipient to get a specific amount of money or a particular bequest, it is generally safer to make the gift tax-free and leave the tax to be paid out of the residue. If your bequests and legacies exceed £231,000 you should take legal advice.

If you're making a large bequest (such as a house, farm or business), or bequests which add up to a fair proportion of your estate, making them tax-free could eat up the residue. Making the large bequests after-tax means that the recipient pays the bill – you could help with this by taking out a life insurance policy which pays the recipient enough when you die to pay the estimated tax bill (see page 10).

A large tax-free legacy of money could have the same effect of eating up the residue unless you have made a legacy subject to its own inheritance tax. Either make the legacy after-tax (the recipient can draw on the legacy to pay the tax), or leave a share of the residue instead.

The residue

The residue is what is left after all the bequests and legacies have been made and all debts, fees and expenses and other costs have been paid. Any tax payable out of the estate comes out of the residue, and what's left goes to the 'residuary legatee(s)' that you specify in the will.

You can leave the residue to one person (your husband or wife, for example, or a friend). Or it can be divided among several people: you can name the people who are to get it (A, B and C); or you can leave it to a group of people such as your children. The shares can be equal or in stated proportions or percentages.

When the residue is to be left entirely to one or more named people, you can specify alternatives if any of them dies before you. For example, the share of anyone who dies before you could go to his or her children equally; or to someone else; or 'shall accrue to the other residuary legatees'. If you do not specify alternatives, any part of the residue left to a person who is dead will be distributed according to the laws of intestacy rather than being divided up amongst the others named.

When leaving the residue to your husband or wife, make sure you specify alternative arrangements – since there is a chance of you both dying together (in a car accident, say). If the residue goes to your husband or wife only if he or she survives you by a set time (often 30 days), you risk losing the benefit of the nil rate band of inheritance tax on the first death.

Charities and other good causes

Bequests and legacies to charities and certain other clearly defined good causes are free of inheritance tax (see page 6). If leaving something to charity, make sure you get the name right: don't confuse, for example, the Cancer Research Campaign with the Imperial Cancer Research Fund. Ask the charity for exact details of what to put, including the address.

Express the legacy as: 'I give £200 to the Wombat Preservation Trust and the receipt of the secretary or treasurer, or other person professing to be the proper officer for the time being, shall be sufficient discharge to my executors.' This protects the executors, who can produce such a receipt to prove that they have paid the money to the right people.

Certain types of 'heritage property' (e.g. land in a beauty spot, historic houses and works of art) can be free of inheritance tax if left for the public benefit. But special complicated rules apply – get professional advice.

Drawing up your will

We have devised four simple will forms for you to use in drawing up your own will. Choose the one most suitable for your needs. If you wish to make any amendments or additions you and your witnesses should initial the alteration(s) when you sign the will.

If your estate exceeds the inheritance tax limit, consider taking legal advice on how to minimise inheritance tax before making your will.

Use the flowchart below to decide which to use.

START HERE

Is your permanent home in England or Wales?

NO

If you are domiciled elsewhere (e.g. Scotland, Ireland or abroad) you should not use this Pack, even if you are currently living in England or Wales, unless you own property or land in England and Wales.

YES

Is your total estate likely to exceed the inheritance tax limit? (Don't forget gifts and inheritances.)

YES

Consider taking legal advice – this could result in significant savings of inheritance tax.

NO

Are you leaving the residue to your spouse and then to your children?

YES

Are any of the children under 18?

NO

Use the GREEN will form (this can be used to leave your estate to other adults as well with suitable amendments).

YES

Use the YELLOW will form. The trustees' power to invest is restricted unless the power is extended. Trustees can release only half the capital for the benefit of the child unless the power is extended.

NO

Do you want to leave everything to one person or institution?

YES

Use the BLUE will form (the substitutional gift can be deleted if your original gift is to one or more charities).

NO

Use the RED will form to leave various legacies and then to divide the residue between several people or charities (delete the space for legacies if you only want to dispose of the residue).

Blue will

Use this if you wish to leave everything to one or more persons or institutions (i.e. with no other bequests or legacies). If you're leaving everything to a child under 18, using the blue will means that the estate will be administered according to the strict rules of the trustee laws (see page 12). Remember to make clear what happens if the first beneficiary dies before you.

Red will

Use this if you want to leave several bequests or legacies (even if some of them are fairly small). Anything left to a child under 18 will be administered according to the strict rules of the trustee laws unless they are relaxed in the will.

Yellow will

Use this if you wish to leave the estate to your child (or children) under 18, whether as first choice or as the alternative if the first choice dies before you, *and* want to give the trustees more flexibility than the restrictive trustee laws. This yellow will allows trustees to keep property such as land and homes, to invest in any income-producing investment they think suitable and to hand money over to the children's guardians (to buy a bigger home if needed). It also lets you specify an age later than 18 for your children to get their shares of the inheritance.

Green will

If you want to leave everything to your spouse, or to your adult children if your spouse dies before you.

If none of these four wills suits your needs take professional advice. This applies, for example, if you want to set up a trust for your spouse or children.

In section 10 we give examples of how our will forms can be completed for a variety of circumstances. Look through the examples to see how different objectives can be achieved in filling in the drafts.

How to fill in the forms

Fill in the details as set out in Worksheet B in the spaces on the will forms.

Write clearly, printing in capitals if your writing is hard to read. Avoid crossing out or alterations (and certainly don't use typewriter correction fluid). Three copies of each of our will forms are supplied: use one to do a rough draft first before making the real thing (destroy the rough draft to avoid confusion).

Use clear and precise plain English – avoid passive or conditional tenses. Don't try to use what you imagine to be legal jargon. And never assume that people will know what you mean: they may not, and in any case, the will must be interpreted on the basis of what it says, not what you intended. Be watchful for conflicting wishes. For example, do not give the house to your spouse and then say what is to happen to it on his/her death, unless you intend to create a life trust.

Describe beneficiaries, executors and everyone else as fully as possible, to avoid confusion. 'Mr and Mrs Jones' alone could be open to debate; so could (even) 'my parents' if either has remarried. 'My parents Bob and Ann Jones' would be much better: always try to mention both the relationship to you and the person's full name.

If any of the boxes in our forms are too big, fill up the empty space as illustrated for Alison Brown's will on page 27. If any of the gaps aren't big enough, you can type out – or very clearly write – your own will. Copy the wording of our forms carefully without mistakes or alterations. Do not leave blank spaces and try to keep it to one side of paper. If the will goes to two pages, continue on the back of the first sheet rather than starting a fresh sheet (so that nothing can be added on the blank side later).

Number each page, for example 'page 2 of 3'. Make sure that some of the will appears on the last side (i.e. don't leave just the signatures and the accompanying clause on a page by themselves).

SECTION 8

Signing your will

Witnesses

You need two people to witness you signing the will (you don't have to show them what's in it). They should not be blind or under 18 or mentally incapacitated. The witnesses should not be left anything in the will, nor should their husband or wife. If they are, they lose what's given by the will (although the will remains validly witnessed) – their share falls into the residue.

Both witnesses must be present together with you when you sign the will. They must each sign it immediately after you below your signature, with you still there. Never use rubber stamps to print signatures – all the signatures must be by hand.

If the will covers more than one page, sign the bottom of each side in the witnesses' presence and they should sign also. If there are any alterations, initial them in the witnesses' presence, and get them to add their initials. If you have drawn lines to fill up blank spaces, initial these at the top and bottom in the presence of the witnesses, who should add their initials in each place (see the example of Alison Brown's will on page 27).

After signing the will

Don't pin anything on the will, or staple sheets together or use a paperclip to hold them together – it might later look as if something attached had been removed. Find a safe place to keep the will and tell relatives where it is. Tell them where the original is and let them know if you want to be buried or cremated (in case the will is not read until after the funeral). We've supplied a readily identifiable envelope to keep your will in, together with your 'What do you own?' questionnaire which will help your executors sort things out.

If there's nowhere safe at home, you can ask your bank to look after your will (they'll normally charge a fee). Take a copy to keep at home, with a note attached saying where the original is. Alternatively, you can deposit your will at the Principal Registry, Family Division, Record Keepers Department, Somerset House, Strand, London WC2R 1LP (tel. 0171-936 7000). This costs £1. A pre-printed envelope containing the required wording can be obtained from the nearest probate registry, either by writing or, if it is a district office, by calling in person.

Reviewing your will

Review your will frequently - every three to five years, say, or more often. Your circumstances change with time as do those of your family; inflation and tax changes will also have to be taken into account. If an important beneficiary of your will dies, this should also prompt a review.

Follow through the procedures in this Pack fully each time - we have supplied extra copies of each form to help you do this. If you draw up and sign a new will using our drafts, it automatically revokes all previous wills - destroy the old will to help avoid any possible confusion.

Marriage and divorce

In general, marriage automatically revokes previous wills. If you get married, draw up a new will after the ceremony (unless the old will says it was drawn up in contemplation of your marriage and you do actually marry the person the will mentions).

Divorce does not automatically revoke your previous will, but if you have named your spouse as an executor, divorce cancels this out. It also cancels out any bequests or legacies to your former spouse - these now go into residue (if your former spouse was to get the residue, it will be distributed according to the intestacy rules). If you remarry, get professional advice about your will.

Alterations to your will

Any changes to your will after it has been signed and witnessed should be done either by drawing up a new will, or by adding a codicil (which confirms the original will but adds to it). Never write alterations on your will after it has been signed - they have no legal validity, will be ignored and could cause great trouble and expense after your death.

For a straightforward change, a codicil may be simpler than drawing up a new will. The example below shows how you can draw up a simple codicil, which must be witnessed in exactly the same manner as a will itself (although you don't have to use the same people who witnessed your will). Don't staple, clip or pin codicils to your will in case it makes it look as if something else which was part of the will has been removed.

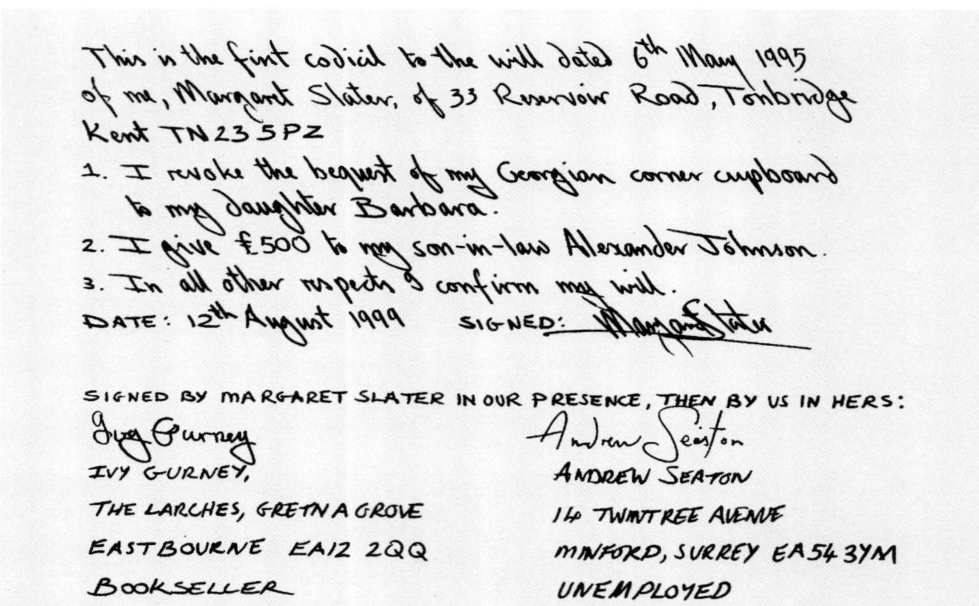
This is the first codicil to the will dated 6th May 1995 of me, Margaret Slater, of 33 Reservoir Road, Tonbridge Kent TN23 5PZ

1. I revoke the bequest of my Georgian corner cupboard to my daughter Barbara.
2. I give £500 to my son-in-law Alexander Johnson.
3. In all other respects I confirm my will.

DATE: 12th August 1999 SIGNED: Margaret Slater

SIGNED BY MARGARET SLATER IN OUR PRESENCE, THEN BY US IN HERS:

Ivy Gurney
IVY GURNEY,
THE LARCHES, GRETNA GROVE
EASTBOURNE EA12 2QQ
BOOKSELLER

Andrew Seaton
ANDREW SEATON
14 TWINTREE AVENUE
MINFORD, SURREY EA54 3YM
UNEMPLOYED

SECTION 10

Examples of completed wills

BLUE WILL

Leaving everything to one person or institution with a substitutional gift if the original beneficiary dies first.

Michael Smith's will

Michael Smith wants to leave everything to his partner, without any other bequests or legacies. If his partner dies before him or at the same time, he wants his estate to be divided up between his two nephews (who are both over 18). He can use the blue will to do this, as illustrated below. His partner should make her will at the same time (and probably in the same terms).

Points

1 Michael gives his *full* name and address.

2 Michael appoints his partner as one executor (since she is due to get the lot) and his friend Henry as the other.

3 Michael leaves everything to his partner but specifies that if she dies before him, his nephews shall divide his estate between them.

MAKE YOUR OWN WILL – AN ACTION PACK FROM WHICH?

Will

WILL TO LEAVE EVERYTHING TO ONE OR MORE PERSONS OR INSTITUTIONS

WILL OF

1

name MICHAEL JOHN SMITH

address 33 ACACIA AVENUE, SLAGTHORPE
BORSET
SQ8 5NY

I revoke all earlier Wills and Codicils.

I APPOINT AS MY EXECUTORS AND TRUSTEES:

2

name	address
MARY LOUISE BROWN	33 ACACIA AVENUE, SLAGTHORPE BORSET SQ8 5NY
HENRY ANDREW SMITH	6 CAMBOURNE DRIVE, SLAGTHORPE BORSET SQ2 3LF

I wish to be ☐ Buried ☐ Cremated (Tick one box)

I LEAVE EVERYTHING I OWN TO:

3

name	address
MARY LOUISE BROWN	33 ACACIA AVENUE, SLAGTHORPE, BORSET SQ8 5NY

BUT IF (IN THE CASE OF INDIVIDUALS) THEY DIE BEFORE ME, I LEAVE EVERYTHING I OWN TO:

name	address
GEORGE PETER GREY	2 YORK ROAD, BRINTON, BORSET SQ3 3PW
ALEXANDER JAMES GREY	2 YORK ROAD, BRINTON, BORSET SQ3 3PW

3

If any of the gifts mentioned in this will are made to charities, my trustees need only obtain a receipt from the person representing that charity who appears to have proper authority.

TESTATOR'S SIGNATURE

sign here [signature] date 26th MARCH 1999

WITNESSES' SIGNATURES

Signed by the person making this will in our presence in whose presence and in the presence of each other we then signed

sign [signature] name PHILIP GREEN
address 30 ACACIA AVENUE, SLAGTHORPE, BORSET occupation SALES EXECUTIVE

sign [signature] name MARJORIE GREEN
address 30 ACACIA AVENUE, SLAGTHORPE, BORSET occupation PHYSIOTHERAPIST

BLUE WILL

Leaving everything to one person or institution with a substitutional gift if the original beneficiary dies first.

Harold Bean's will

Harold Bean is a widower with no children who wishes to leave all his money to his favourite charity. The blue will is ideal for this.

(Although the Imperial Cancer Research Fund is not likely to disappear, you may wish to give an alternative in case the first gift fails for any reason.)

Points

1 Harold gives his *full* name and address.

2 Since he has no close relatives, Harold appoints a close friend as executor.

3 Harold specifies the name and address of the charity to which he wants to leave everything (having checked it by telephone) and uses the charity's form of words to make it clear what his executor needs to do.

4 Two friends witness the will – since all the estate will go to charity, there is no problem with choosing a witness who is not a beneficiary or a spouse of one.

Will

MAKE YOUR OWN WILL – AN ACTION PACK FROM WHICH?

WILL TO LEAVE EVERYTHING TO ONE OR MORE PERSONS OR INSTITUTIONS

WILL OF
name HAROLD BEAN
address THE LARCHES, IVY LANE, BORMINSTER NEWTON
BORSET
SQ8 7PP

I revoke all earlier Wills and Codicils.

I APPOINT AS MY EXECUTORS AND TRUSTEES:

name	address
WILLIAM McGREGOR	47 HIGH STREET, SLAGTHORPE, BORSET SQ8 2RK

I wish to be ☐ Buried ☐ Cremated (Tick one box)

I LEAVE EVERYTHING I OWN TO:

name	address
IMPERIAL CANCER RESEARCH FUND	44, LINCOLN'S INN FIELDS, LONDON WC2A 3PX

BUT IF (IN THE CASE OF INDIVIDUALS) THEY DIE BEFORE ME, I LEAVE EVERYTHING I OWN TO:

name	address
H.B G.S. M.T.	H.B G.S. M.T.

If any of the gifts mentioned in this will are made to charities, my trustees need only obtain a receipt from the person representing that charity who appears to have proper authority.

TESTATOR'S SIGNATURE
sign here Harold Bean
date 14th MAY 1999

WITNESSES' SIGNATURES
Signed by the person making this will in our presence in whose presence and in the presence of each other we then signed

sign G. Streeter name GRAHAM STREETER
address CHURCH COTTAGE, IVY LANE, BORMINSTER NEWTON occupation CIVIL SERVANT
sign M. Templeman name MELANIE TEMPLEMAN
address THE OLD FARM, HILL LANE, BORMINSTER NEWTON occupation JOURNALIST

RED WILL

Several bequests and legacies; then what is left to one or more persons or institutions (but no children under 18).

Mary Smith's will

Mary Smith wants to make a number of bequests and legacies, leaving everything else to her friend Michael. If he should die before her, she would like the residue to be divided equally between her two brothers.

Since none of the residue is to go to a minor child, she doesn't need to worry about trustee rules and can use the red will.

Points

1 Mary gives her *full* name and address.

2 Mary appoints her friend Michael and brother David as executors, with her brother Paul as alternative if either drops out. Since the main beneficiary is likely to be Michael, it is sensible to have him as an executor of the will.

3 Mary bequeaths her valuables to one of her nieces, and leaves a cash legacy to another. She also leaves a small sum of money to the NSPCC, of which she has been a life-long supporter.

4 The residue of Mary's estate goes to her friend Michael. But if he dies before her, the residue will be divided equally between her two brothers.

5 Two of Mary's friends witness the will, since they aren't going to get anything from it.

6 Mary may suggest that her friend Michael makes his will at the same time.

Will

MAKE YOUR OWN WILL – AN ACTION PACK FROM WHICH?

WILL TO LEAVE SEVERAL BEQUESTS AND LEGACIES,

then what is left to one or more persons or institutions

1 WILL OF

name MARY LOUISE SMITH

address 33, ACACIA AVENUE, SLAGTHORPE
BORSET
SQ2 4UB

I revoke all earlier Wills and Codicils

2 I APPOINT AS MY EXECUTORS AND TRUSTEES:

name	address
MICHAEL BRADSHAW	33 ACACIA AVENUE, SLAGTHORPE, BORSET SQ2 4UB
DAVID SMITH	6 CAMBOURNE DRIVE, SLAGTHORPE, BORSET SQ2 3LF

BUT IF EITHER OF THEM IS UNABLE TO ACT, I APPOINT IN THAT PERSONS PLACE MY BROTHER PAUL SMITH OF 10 DELLA AVE, BRADPORT, EASTCASTER, BORSET SQ9 3LD

I wish to be ☐ Buried ☐ Cremated (Tick one box)

3 I GIVE THE FOLLOWING LEGACIES OR ITEMS FREE OF TAX:

name	address	item or amount
KATE SMITH	6 CAMBOURNE DRIVE	
	SLAGTHORPE BORSET SQ2 3LF	MY JEWELLERY
JANE SMITH	10 DELLA DR, BRADPORT	
	EASTCASTER BORSET SQ9 3LD	£ 500
NSPCC	42 CURTAIN RD. LONDON EC2A 3NH	£ 1,000

4 MY TRUSTEES SHALL HOLD WHAT IS LEFT OF MY ESTATE ON TRUST TO SELL OR RETAIN IT AND:

A. To pay my debts, funeral expenses and any inheritance tax

B. To pay what is left to the following:

name	address	proportion
MICHAEL BRADSHAW	33 ACACIA AVE, SLAGTHORPE	
	BORSET SQ2 4UB	THE WHOLE

ms MT. GS

ms MT. GS

C. If any of the gifts mentioned in B fails, it shall be added proportionally to those which do not.

D. If any of the legacies of gifts mentioned in this will are made to charities, my trustees need only obtain a receipt from the person representing that charity who appears to have proper authority.

E. If at the date of my death there is no person or institution mentioned in paragraph B to benefit from my will, my trustees shall instead pay what is left as follows:

name	address	proportion
DAVID SMITH	6 CAMBOURNE DRIVE,	
	SLAGTHORPE	HALF
PAUL SMITH	10 DELLA AVE,	
	BRADPORT	HALF

TESTATOR'S SIGNATURE

sign here Mary L. Smith

date 15 JUNE 1999

5 WITNESSES' SIGNATURES

Signed by the person making this will in our presence in whose presence and in the presence of each other we then signed

sign [signature] print name GREGORY STREETER

address 41, GRANT ST., SLAGTHORPE, BORSET SQ2 4PP occupation STEEPLEJACK

sign [signature] print name MURIEL TEMPLMAN

address 30 CHESHAM RISE, SLAGTHORPE, BORSET SQ2 7HN occupation MIDWIFE

YELLOW WILL

Leaving everything to the spouse or to the children (including children under 18) if the spouse dies first.

Henry Brown's will

Henry Brown has three children, all under the age of 18. He will leave everything to his wife Margaret, but if she dies at the same time or before him, he wants his children to inherit.

The will relaxes some of the rules which usually bind the trustees, but if he does not wish to relax those rules, he should strike out the clauses giving additional powers to the trustees (and then both he and the trustees should initial those deletions).

Points

1 Henry gives his *full* name and address.

2 Henry makes his wife sole executor, since she is the person who inherits everything. He then appoints his friends Gordon and Joyce Saunders who will be executors and trustees if his wife dies before him.

3 Peter and Susan Jackson are appointed guardians of Henry's three children up to the age of 18 if both Henry and Margaret should die – Henry has faith in these friends as substitute parents.

4 Henry specifies that his estate should go to his wife, but that if she dies before him, it will be left to his children. If the children are still under 18, the executors will act as trustees. By using this will form, Henry gives his trustees freedom to invest the children's money more or less as if it were their own (if he wanted them to be bound by the strict rules of investment, he would delete the clauses he does not want to use). The relaxation allows them to release the whole (which might be necessary to pay for school fees, for instance).

5 Henry permits his trustees to enter into an agreement to prevent their suffering financial loss if they look after the children. This arrangement must be made with great care.

6 Henry decides that each child shall become entitled to inherit his or her share of the estate upon reaching 21.

7 Two neighbours, not beneficiaries (nor spouses of beneficiaries) of the will, witness Henry's signature.

8 Margaret Brown should make her will at the same time as her husband.

9 If Henry's estate, together with gifts made in the last seven years, exceeds £231,000 (or if it would when added to Margaret's estate) he should seek legal advice before completing a will in order to avoid inheritance tax problems.

Will

MAKE YOUR OWN WILL – AN ACTION PACK FROM WHICH?

WILL TO LEAVE EVERYTHING TO SPOUSE

or to the children **under 18** if the spouse dies first

1 WILL OF

name HENRY DAVID BROWN

address 9 FALMOUTH CRESCENT, SLAGTHORPE
BORSET
SQ6 4AS

2 I revoke all earlier Wills and Codicils.

I give the whole of my estate to my ~~husband~~/wife (name) MARGARET ANN BROWN

and appoint ~~him~~/her my sole executor.

I wish to be ☐ Buried ☑ Cremated (Tick one box)

If my ~~husband~~/wife dies before me the following provisions shall apply:

I APPOINT AS MY EXECUTORS AND TRUSTEES:

name	address
GORDON SAUNDERS	22 PENZANCE DRIVE, SLAGTHORPE BORSET SQ3 8GH
JOYCE SAUNDERS	22 PENZANCE DRIVE, SLAGTHORPE BORSET SQ3 8GH

3 I APPOINT AS THE GUARDIANS OF MY INFANT CHILDREN

name	address
~~RETER~~ PETER JACKSON	18 FISHERMAN'S BEND SLAGTHORPE, BORSET SQ38YD
SUSAN JACKSON	18 FISHERMAN'S BEND SLAGTHORPE, BORSET SQ38YD

HDB PJ SJ HDB. PD SJ

4 MY TRUSTEES SHALL HOLD MY ESTATE ON TRUST TO SELL OR RETAIN IT AND:

A. To pay my debts, funeral expenses and any inheritance tax.

B. To pay what is left to the following children in the following proportions providing they survive me and attain: ☐ 18 ☑ 21. (Tick one box)

name	address	proportion
GODFREY BROWN	9 FALMOUTH CRESCENT	ONE THIRD
DAVID BROWN	9 FALMOUTH CRESCENT	ONE THIRD
ANN BROWN	9 FALMOUTH CRESCENT	ONE THIRD

B.B. HDB TB
HDB T.B B.B.

5 If any of my children (of whatever age) die before me leaving children who attain 18, those children shall share the benefit which their parent would have had if they had not died before me but if any of the gifts above should fail they shall be added proportionally to those which do not.

6 I GIVE THE FOLLOWING ADDITIONAL POWERS TO MY TRUSTEES:

A. To invest as freely as they could if my money was their own.

B. To apply for the benefit of any beneficiary who is under ☐ 18 ☑ 21 (Tick one box) the whole or any part of the capital to which he is or may become entitled.

C. To enter into a financial agreement with the guardians of my infant children in order to enable the guardians to provide the best possible care for my children without financial loss to the guardians but my trustees shall not be liable for any resulting loss to my estate providing they have not been reckless or dishonest.

TESTATOR'S SIGNATURE

sign here H D Brown date 11 May 1999

7 WITNESSES' SIGNATURES

Signed by the person making this will in our presence in whose presence and in the presence of each other we then signed

sign Bruce Bloomfield name BRUCE BLOOMFIELD
address 7 FALMOUTH CRESCENT, SLAGTHORPE, BORSET occupation COMPUTER PROGRAMMER

sign Tracey Bloomfield name TRACEY BLOOMFIELD
address 7 FALMOUTH CRESCENT, SLAGTHORPE, BORSET occupation HOUSEWIFE

GREEN WILL

Your own children over 18 are major beneficiaries if your spouse dies before you. The green will could also be used (with suitable amendments) if you had no children but wished to leave your estate to other beneficiaries if your spouse died before you.

Alison Brown's will

Alison Brown is married with two grown-up children. If she dies she wants her estate to go to her husband, but if he dies before her she wants to leave her estate to her son and daughter.

Points

1 Alison gives her *full* name and address.

2 Alison makes her husband the sole executor as he gets the whole of her estate if she dies before him.

3 Alison appoints her son and daughter as her executors in the event of her husband dying before her.

4 If Alison wanted to leave any legacies or specific items, she could consider using the red will.

5 Alison asks some friends to witness the will, since they are not going to benefit from it.

MAKE YOUR OWN WILL – AN ACTION PACK FROM WHICH?

Will

WILL TO LEAVE EVERYTHING TO SPOUSE

then to other beneficiaries including children **over 18** if the spouse dies first

WILL OF

1 name ALISON MARILYN BROWN
address 88 AUGUSTUS DRIVE, SLAGTHORPE
BORSET
SQ8 9WJ

I revoke all earlier Wills and Codicils.

Gift to spouse

2 I give the whole of my estate to my ~~wife~~/husband (name) JULIAN BROWN
and appoint ~~her~~/him my sole executor.

I wish to be ☐ Buried ☑ Cremated (Tick one box)

If my ~~wife~~/husband dies before me the following provisions shall apply:

I APPOINT AS MY EXECUTORS AND TRUSTEES: 3

name	address
ANTHONY BROWN	HEAM HOUSE, BRIGHTHORPE, BORSET SQ9 4LK
HELEN HOAR	155 TOWER WAY, SLAGTHORPE, BORSET SQ9 5TY

AB. DB MB AB. MB DB

MY TRUSTEES SHALL HOLD MY ESTATE ON TRUST TO SELL OR RETAIN IT AND:

A. To pay my debts, funeral expenses and any inheritance tax.

B. To pay what is left as follows:

Gift of residue to children or (with suitable amendments initialled by the testator and the witnesses) to other beneficiaries

name	address	proportion
ANTHONY BROWN	HEAM HOUSE	HALF
HELEN HOAR	155 TOWER WAY	HALF

AB. MB DB AB. DB MB

If any of my children mentioned above die before me leaving children those children shall share the benefit which their parent would have had if they had outlived me, but if any of the gifts above should fail, they shall be added proportionally to those which do not.

TESTATOR'S SIGNATURE

sign here Alison Brown date 20th JULY 1999

WITNESSES' SIGNATURES 5

Signed by the person making this will in our presence in whose presence and in the presence of each other we then signed

sign D Banks name DAVID BANKS
address 4, HEDGES ROW, SLAGTHORPE, BORSET SQ9 3ET occupation BANK MANAGER
sign M Banks name MARIANNE BANKS
address 4, HEDGES ROW, SLAGTHORPE BORSET SQ9 3ET occupation SCHOOLTEACHER

OTHER WHICH? PUBLICATIONS

THE WHICH? GUIDE TO PENSIONS

Getting unbiased advice on the best pension is crucial given the range of options and the fear of joining a poor scheme. This easy-to-follow guide helps you plan effectively and make the right choice for your situation, taking into account Budget changes, government plans for a new state pension, and stakeholder pensions. How much to save, and how much the state will provide; special measures for those facing redundancy or divorce; employers' schemes and what to do when you change jobs; alternative savings schemes – all are covered, with examples, charts and a glossary of 'pensionspeak'.

THE WHICH? GUIDE TO GIVING AND INHERITING

Gifts left in wills are all too often diminished by unnecessary tax bills, or available tax relief is not taken up. Even the smallest bequest can cause avoidable tax problems for your heirs. Using handy calculators and examples of typical situations, this guide shows how knowledge of the tax rules can ensure that your bequests are as large as you intend, that your home and possessions are passed on intact, and that the beneficiaries are those whom you wish to receive your gifts.

THE WHICH? GUIDE TO AN ACTIVE RETIREMENT

Retirement is a time for new challenges and to develop new skills - a beginning, not an end, and a time to redefine your life. This book covers financial planning in detail, including maximising your pension and other sources of income, managing your tax affairs, and passing on your money tax-efficiently. Topics covered include continuing work, whether paid, voluntary or starting a small business; keeping fit, eating well and coping with common health pension planning for those with dependants; problems; where to live; holidays and leisure; and caring for elderly relatives.

WHAT TO DO WHEN SOMEONE DIES

Including advice on arranging your own funeral in case you wish to plan ahead and avoid later worry, this book guides people through the process of making the practical arrangements that are necessary after a death, from registration to funerals and organ donation.

These Which? Consumer Guides, plus many other titles, are available by post from Which? Books, Castlemead, Gascoyne Way, Hertford X, SG14 1LH (post and packing free), and through bookshops. Credit card holders can ring their order FREE to Consumers' Association on 0800-252100 quoting their Mastercard or Visa number.

Contents of back pocket

Worksheet A: What do you own? (2 copies)

Worksheet B: What do you want to put in your will? (2 copies)

Blue will form: For one or more beneficiaries (3 copies)

Red will form: For several legatees and residuary beneficiaries (3 copies)

Yellow will form: To provide for a spouse and then children including any children under 18 (3 copies)

Green will form: To provide for a spouse, then adult children or other beneficiaries (3 copies)

An envelope to store your completed will.